A Beginner's Guide to Disaster Management

Survival kits, 72 hour Kits and Disaster Control Tips

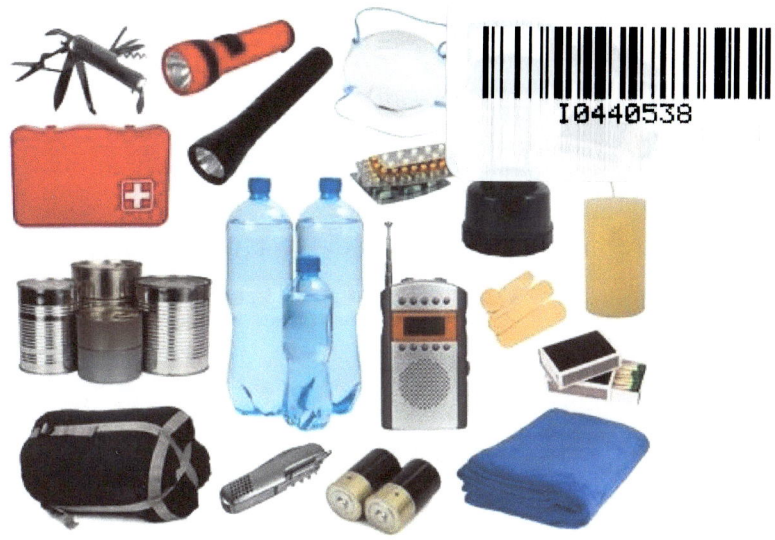

Prepping and Survival Books

Dueep Jyot Singh

Mendon Cottage Books

JD-Biz Publishing

Download Free Books!

http://MendonCottageBooks.com

All Rights Reserved

Our books are available at

1. Amazon.com
2. Barnes and Noble
3. Itunes
4. Kobo
5. Smashwords
6. Google Play Books

Table of Contents

Introduction

This book is all about survival – survival of the fittest, survival during man-made and natural calamities and catastrophes, and how to cope with disaster.

I will be telling you about historical and present-day examples in this book, about disaster management and about attitudes of people when faced with disaster. So this book is just not about managing a disaster on a personal level, it is How about coping and being prepared for disaster when and where it strikes.

The 21st century, unfortunately, with its state-of-the-art technology and technical development is one of the most dangerous eras in the history of mankind. However much we talk about world peace, we know in our hearts of hearts that that will never happen, because then man will not have anything else on which to quarrel and argue with his fellow man.

Good sense has never been the first priority of mankind when ambition and greed and ulterior motives of *Ich Uber Alles* lurks in the hearts of men. And that is his first instinct, conquer, rule, and destroy.

Apart from man-made catastrophes, unfortunately, Nature has also begun to take a hand in the process of destruction. And she is more powerful than 1000 nuclear bombs. In fact, she is quite capable of putting man in his tiny little space in her scheme of things. So one may survive the wrath of man against man, but one is rather helpless when faced with nature in all her destructive splendor and glory.

And that is why man has to use his good sense to face reality and understand that his family and his survival depends on a little bit of strategic planning, right now, when he has the time and means to gather unto himself the necessary things which can mean life and death, for he and his family.

Now what made me decide to write on survival with tips and techniques?

I was rather surprised, when I went to a friend's house, and saw that she had four bags packed and placed at strategic exits. When she saw me looking at them, quizzically, she just told me, "Oh, those are just our family survival kits. It is better to be safer than to be sorry and to be caught napping and unprepared."

I came back home and began to think. Now, here was a clearheaded family, who knew that disaster could strike anywhere, anytime. Besides, we live in an area, which is prone to earthquakes. Waking up in the middle of the night, to find our ceiling trembling is part and parcel of our lives and we have got used to it. Also, we know that one fine day, it may literally and figuratively fall on us.

An ostrich attitude is definitely not a sensible attitude to take in this day and age of disasters – natural and man-made. You never know when you will need to survive in a world, which is definitely not the one in which you spent the days of your youth.

Facing Disaster down the Ages

Here I am talking about one of the basic realities of human life – every generation down the ages has faced, and will have to face war, because it is human nature. So however much we may talk about world peace, which can never happen. One has to face this. And one has also to face the fact that world wars can start because someone decides that he needs to spread the borders of his country and the rest of the world says that it is the none of their business trying to stop him.

There is going to be somebody, somewhere, flexing his muscles and invading sovereign states under no excuse whatsoever and the rest of the world will keep saying, as long as we are not affected, why bother.

History shows that people know that disaster is around the corner, but they do not want to accept this fact. This proof is during the Second World War, when the British politicians kept on persisting Peace in our Times, even though they saw the countries around them being invaded by the armies of a power-hungry megalomaniac.

History may hide the fact that some British politicians spoke to Hitler's council, which they were willing to surrender with a government in a state of partial autonomy. They definitely did not ask the advice of Parliament or even their people about this decision made to save their own skins. But thanks to Winston Churchill, who decided No Surrender No Slavery, Britons will never be slaves, Hitler did not manage to conquer the people of this land.

But the damage had been done. When war was declared between Britain and Germany in 1939, those cowardly politicians who would rather stay safe and see their country falling under the foot of tyrants had already done the damage. No army, no supplies, no food, no ammunition.

They did not want to prepare for war, because that would show that they were preparing for aggression. Besides, Britain has always followed the policy of this cannot happen to us. They did not learn from the Zulu wars, the Boer war, the Crimean War and the Indian Mutiny of 1857 and now sending troops and supplies to Iraq, which they can ill afford even though their financial economy is in a mess.

Matter of pride always loses over good sense and they keep spending pounds in cures, when an ounce of prevention would have prevented all that problem and trouble.

According to them, *if they never prepared for war, it would never come to them.* But they did not have to go seeking a war.

On the other hand, they have always been caught napping in times of war even though people of good sense kept telling them that political situations in their colonies presaged war and disaster.

According to them, they had this feeling – this cannot happen to us, we are British and we rule the world. Nobody can fight against us.

In the 21st century, it is. Let us go to war and make our people concentrate on a supposed enemy rather than concentrate and question us on the terrible situation right at home. This has been done down the centuries by politicians, kings, emperors and now by political advisers.

Those days of world conquest should have been gone, but there are countries who still persist on making nuisances of themselves all over the world. But if war comes to their own country, I would not be surprised if they find themselves complaining, "well, how did that happen? We did not expect it. This cannot happen to us. We are supposed to be the most powerful countries in this region, how can we be invaded by some other country?"

But it has happened, and it will happen again.

Wars are an inevitable part of the human social fabric and psyche

I read a book written by a British writer named Lucilla Andrews called <u>Frontline 1940,</u> in which an American visiting Britain in the early days of the war – the Battle of Britain – is perplexed at their attitude of carry on, Nevertheless, after the disaster of Dunkirk.

With Winston Churchill at the helm, and telling his countrymen that he had no intention of suing for peace with the Germans, here is the paragraph which I quote from the book.

"... I have not figured out what makes the English tick. Arrogance? Stupidity? No imagination? The security of being islanders? Just a blank crazy faith in themselves? The lot? Or whatever. Whatever, there is nothing – repeat, nothing – that boosts their more like having their backs the wall, and that is where they right now they have just – repeat, yes – cottoned on. This right little tight little island only got around to taking it a mite seriously when they had to get their guys out from under at Dunkirk. Like I said they kind of like to take their time."

This attitude may look praiseworthy in the 1940s because at that time, they had their backs to the wall. The British were lulled into that sort of false security that nothing would happen to them because their politicians had promised them peace in their times. So when war came, it was what do we do now?

One is rather horrified when one reads about the incompetency, bad planning and loss of precious lives and material at Dunkirk. But man will never learn from his mistakes. He will allow other people to dictate his life for him, because he prefers the line of least resistance. People of other nations just stand by and watch the fun. This is holding up that particular country's progress, they declaring war, all the better for us. Can we sell them some outdated arms?

And that is why wars are still being fought in the 21st century

It was just by chance that the air attacks over Britain in 1940 stopped when they did. One more week and Britain would have to go in for unconditional surrender.

Even after all Churchill had said on the subject, it is not known whether the British people realize what would have happened had the RAF lost the battle of Britain. If the ill-equipped remains of the regular Army, the similarly ill-equipped and still largely untrained conscripted Army, and the hundreds of thousands of volunteer, amateur, grossly ill-equipped part-time soldiers had had to take on the superbly trained, equipped and professional Wehrmacht , nothing could have saved the British mainland from German occupation in 1940.[1]

Now this is a matter of a governmental decision. When you face disaster and calamity on your personal level, you have to make all the decisions. It is how well you are prepared personally mentally, spiritually, physically and emotionally to face disaster that is going to make all the difference between the survival of your family and giving up.

We cannot afford to have that What am I to do, someone please help me attitude, languid lily, Barbara Cartland heroine type attitude, – praying for

---

[1]

http://lyricsplayground.com/alpha/songs/c/couldyoupleaseobligeuswithabrengun.shtml

This is the real situation in 1943 immortalized by Noel Coward – can you please send us a Bren gun. The Ministry of supply was woefully unable to meet the demands of the regular army , let alone the Home guard. The disaster preparedness of governments in many other countries, even today, is still in this condition and is in no state to face natural disasters and man-made disasters.

her dead mother to come save her, instead of lifting a hand to help herself –
in war or peace in the 21st century. One needs to be practical. Disaster can
strike anywhere, and "This cannot happen to me," is definitely not an
attitude, which a person can afford to take in this age of natural and human
produced disasters.

So, it is in your interest that you look at the Boy Scouts motto of "Be
prepared" and get survival kits ready for your family.

First of all, you need to look at the products which are going to go into your
survival kits.

Getting To Know More about Survival Kits

 For people living in earthquake prone zones, a disaster survival kit needs to be an integral part of your family evacuation and emergency preparation plan.

Seismic disasters can strike anywhere; so do not imagine that the government is capable of getting to you in time, in case of a natural catastrophe. This is why you need your own disaster kit.

You may have to rely on yourself and your own personal resources, for at least a couple of hours before government agencies appear to help and evacuate the earthquake victims. You can consider this to be a worst case scenario; so get your earthquake kits along with the first aid supplies ready and placed in strategic places, to be used during an emergency evacuation situation

So what are the important items which should be present in a disaster survival kit?

Remember that a survival kit is definitely not restricted to just earthquakes; a disaster survival kit can be used during a terrorist attack, brush fire, hurricane, tornado, house fire, flood, or any sort of situation in which there is a loss of water and electricity availability.

Get your earthquake kit ready with these essential items in it –

The size of the kit is going to depend upon the size of your family. So, look at this list of items placed in your own personalized survival kit and start ticking your list.

For Warmth and Shelter

Clothes, according to the weather, lightweight rain guard, tube tent, lightweight space blanket for warmth, heavy gloves and shoes.

Magnifying glass for lighting fires, waterproof matches, lighter, and butane fuel, and torches with battery. You can also add PLBs (personal locator beacon), candles, flashlights, compasses, paper and pens, and a map for signaling purposes to the kit.

When I was making up my survival kit, I just remember to add something which people may find rather amusing. But this is practical. I added three spools of an amazingly strong hundred percent nylon thread, which I normally use for art and craft beading purposes. After that, I added a good pair of scissors, a surgical blade, and a needle threader. You may ask me why I added this nylon thread instead of ordinary cotton thread for sewing and clothes repairing purposes.

That is because this thread looks as fine as cotton thread, but try as I might, I could not break it by my hands, even though I tried doing so with all my might and main. I had to snip it off with scissors. So, being rather creative, I used that thread instead of ordinary cotton thread to repair some torn clothes, in places which had a tendency to tear – the seat region – and that thread held that fabric so well, that I now use that thread for repairing every single piece of torn cloth, irrespective of fabric or portion torn.

Cotton thread is good enough for delicate hemming or color coordinated stitching on your clothes. But this sturdy, nearly invisible thread is excellent for repairing clothes.

You may want to see what it is like – here.

http://www.ebay.com/itm/4380-yards-0-1mm-Quilter-s-invisible-100-nylon-monofilament-thread-/231106917108?pt=LH_DefaultDomain_0&var=&hash=item35cf0bb2f4

Do not go by the price. That is exorbitant. You can get better bargains online, or in shops in your city. But you know exactly what you need to buy. I bought my hundred yards spool- it said hundred percent nylon fishing yarn – for an equivalent of USD.25 at an art and crafts shop. I just said I needed very thin nylon thread for sequin and bead threading along with threading needles.

http://www.ebay.com/itm/1-500-YARDS-1-371M-BONDED-NYLON-THREAD-69-TEX70-SEW-LEATHER-CANVAS-UPHOLSTERY-/121142230451?pt=LH_DefaultDomain_0&var=&hash=item1c34a3bdb3

This URL is just for your reference, if you want to buy this thread for other heavy-duty purposes! These auctions will probably end by the time you read this book so just search for "Quilter's invisible 100% nylon monofilament thread"

You may want to give every responsible member of the family a well working lighter. Not only is an excellent weapon of defense, – instant fire in your hands – but also, it is going to be good to help keep your family warm, especially when there is no heat or electricity-based warming source.

Learn how to replace the lighter liquid in the lighter from a professional. And then put in a plastic bottle of lighter fluid in your pack.

First Aid Supply

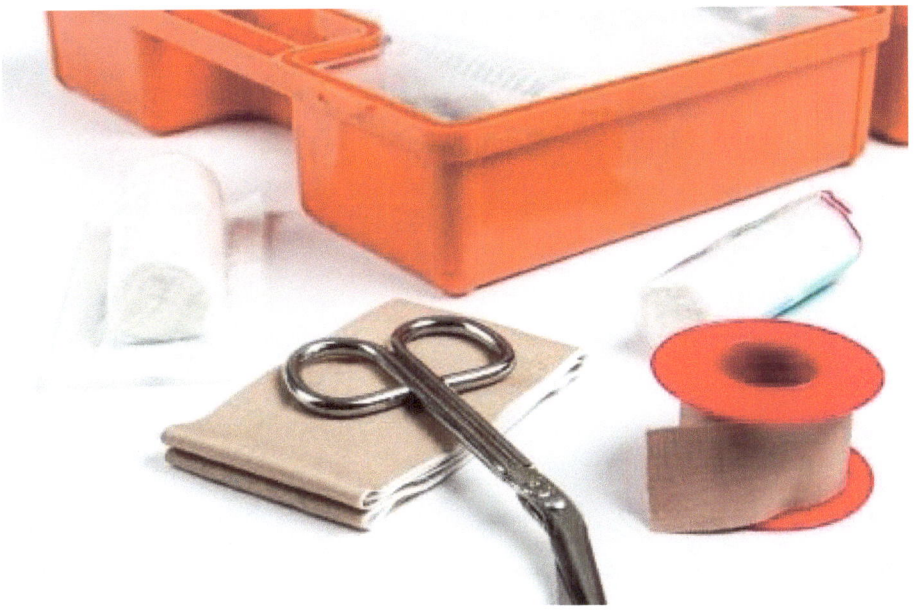

Your first aid kit is going to have sterile gauze, bandages and first aid tape, scissors, disinfectants, Ibuprofen and oxytetracycline. Include soap, feminine personal hygiene products and insect repellent.

The important first-aid supplies include antiseptic creams and sprays, burn ointment, tweezers and a microspore bandage sticking plaster roll, which can be cut without the help of scissors.

I love this plaster roll, which I saw being used extensively in my cousin's 30 bed hospital. You just use a disinfectant to clean any cut, put a piece of clean cotton around it, grab this roll, bandage the affected area and pull away. The nicest thing about this plaster roll is that even an eight-year-old child can do the bandaging, without resorting to scissors. That is because the material tears away so easily.

After that, you need to look at essential drugs, which would include analgesics, antibacterial drugs, antifungal medicines, and of course, a regularly updated supply of all the scheduled drugs used by your family members, if any.

Do You Need Identification Tags?

Identification tags are a part of Army life, and they being practical made sure that every soldier had these tags around his neck. I do not know how easily available tags, just like these are in your area, but at least have something with information about your name, your address, emergency phone number, person to contact in case of an emergency, visible identification marks in your body – to prove that you are who you are, – blood group, diabetic or nondiabetic and allergies to any medicines upon your body at all times.

During the Second World War, the Nazis ordered all the soldiers and officers to be tattooed with their blood group, on their arms. That is so that the doctors could just lift up the arm of an unconscious soldier or officer, say, well, , bring a bottle of B+ blood and set up the IV drip, whilst I get to him.

Ironically, this tattooing was one of the ways in which German officers were identified after their defeat in 1944, and they had started to escape to South America to escape reprisals and judgment at Nuremberg.

They had to get these tattoos removed by a plastic surgeon and often, the plastic surgeon wondered casually in the hearing of Allied, American and Russian officers why that South American Senor , who was in their country for business purposes wanted a tattoo removed from his upper arm.

And bingo, another war criminal who could not resist peeping out of his shell instead of lying low would be trapped.

But getting your children's arms tattooed with their blood groups is rather drastic. They are not in the military. They are just ordinary human beings who need to learn how to survive in possible disaster situations.

Preparing Your 72 Hour Kit

It takes anywhere between 48 to 72 hours for government services in the East to wake up the fact that disaster has struck somewhere.[2] Until then, the people of that area are on their own. And that time is spent by the politicians visiting the area with accompanying news hounds, and allocating funds to be given to the affected people, instead of asking the general administration to set about rescuing the families affected.

Many countries of the East are definitely ill-prepared for disaster management. That is because they have an ostrich attitude about this cannot happen to us. And when it happens, they are found fluttering about completely bewildered and flustered, talking, promising financial help and wasting time instead of making sensible decisions and employing their time more effectively by sending or utilizing manual practical help.

Disaster relief processes in the US and other parts of the West are much more efficient and streamlined, but even under some circumstances, they may not be able to reach you within 48 hours. That is why you have to make up a 72 hour kit for every member of the family, so that you can survive.

---

[2] http://en.wikipedia.org/wiki/2013_North_India_floods

However, the administration is not always caught napping – these people were evacuated before Phailin struck. Human life lost was minimal. That was because the general administration took warning systems of a cyclone striking, seriously, beforehand.

Http://www.nytimes.com/2013/10/13/world/asia/india-cyclone.html?_r=0

In many Asian countries like Thailand and India, rescue work is done by the Army.

Food and water for a 72 hour kit includes water purifying iodine tablets and salt for food, canned foods, tin can opener and fishing tools.

Sleeping bags for every family member, extra clothes, both for winter and for summer, blankets, canvas shoes (keds) and socks, water purifying tablets, flashlights with battery, personal hygiene products, rainproof bedding and covering, high calorie long lasting food bars, flashlights, multipurpose knife and easily ignited fuel tablets, along with a lighter are just some of the important things which need to be added to your survival kit.

Some people also put in portable radios with a long-lasting battery in the kit.

A good survival kit can be considered to be a 72 hour kit, because you need to suppose yourself cut away from rescue operations in about this time limit. This is of course the worst-case scenario, but 3 days is the bare minimum of time for which you need to be prepared.

Medical prescriptions, along with the dosage as well as important family papers, like certificates, passports, driving license, etc. can also be stored away in the survival kits. Also put in some ready cash and credit cards in the kit.

Now you need to look at the water supply. Each family member needs at least one gallon of water, every day. So you need easy access to stored water, kept away from the sunlight.

Here are some other multipurpose items which you can add to the kit --
needles and threads, cable saws for cutting wood, 550 strength parachute
cord, multipurpose hobo or Swiss knife and of course, protective firearms
with corresponding ammunition.

When I asked my friend's husband why he had packed the Army knife and
protective firearms, because he was basically a peaceful person and he had
seen grim war, he said, "I am going to take this disaster situation to be a
Code red situation." [In the East, code red means war.] "Everybody is going
to want to escape that area. They are going to grab supplies from the weaker
members of society. I have two daughters. I have taught them that losing
their supplies means the difference between life and death. So I have taught
them to protect them. And that includes threatening potential robbers with a
knife. I will use the firearms, because I have a license and I am better trained
to do that. At that time, the law and order situation is going to break down. It
is going to be every man for himself. And matters can escalate badly if your
family is left unprotected. And all their passports are also up to date. "

Why Passports?

He said that he was being practical. He was going to find the easiest way of getting out of the country, if there was civil war and ethnic cleansing was in the political agenda.

People in many parts of the West are not worried about this particular part of man-made catastrophe and disaster. But there are many parts of the world, where everybody lives with this fear of potential calamity, especially they belong to a minority religion or caste or race.

I know about an army officer who bought open tickets for Australia for all the members of his family and has been holding them for the last 30 years after the mass genocide against people of his religion in 1984 in India.

Even though he is a serving Army officer and so is not allowed to go abroad, he says that when madness strikes and when there is political clout behind it, nobody bothers about whether a person is a serving high-ranking officer or not – he belongs to a hated religion. He has to be destroyed. At that time, it is practical to leave everything behind and take your family away from a hate ridden country, even though it is your own.

Nobody is going to help you at that time. Crystal Night before the Second World War was the presage of things to come. Those who woke up and read the writing on the wall left Germany while they could. Those who were left behind got gassed in Auswitz and Dachau.

History tries to hide the fact that this cleansing was not limited to people belonging to one race. It was also done to old people, handicapped children and children who were not perfectly built to the idea of that perfect Aryan.

These handicapped and crippled children were German and Christian. And their parents did not protest against such a cleansing, because it was their fault their child was not genetically perfect.

You can put in an emergency cell phone, along with the recharging cord and batteries in the kit. Also put in a list of important phone numbers to contact in case of an emergency, in your disaster kit. Keep the cell phone charged and keep renewing the items in the kit every month, after a complete inspection.

 A little bit of effort now in the making up of your earthquake survival kit is going to save you a lot of hassle during a possible future catastrophe.

Survival – Psychological Effect Of a Disaster

Man is psychologically built not to accept reality when it comes in the shape of a disaster. That is because he needs hope to survive. Even though he sees his house and land being washed away in floods, or being buried under tons of earth, his mind in survival mode is going to say – "when I come back and we start re-building again, this is what I am going to do." That is the sign of a healthy outlook. That is when he is strong enough to think positively. However that is rarely the case.

Many people, when faced with disaster for the first time in their lives are quite content to curl up in a ball and moan about their days of glory and prosperity. Why do we admire Scarlett O Hara so? She definitely did not sit down in a rocking chair, and dream of the days when she was the belle of the area. She went to work. She knew that her world had been destroyed. It would not come back. On the other hand, it depended on her to make something better out of what she was facing today – reality.

And she survived. On the other hand, I know about many women who would rather garner the pity and sympathy of their relatives because they faced a disaster. These women sit on rocking chairs, with their arms folded, moaning plaintively about all the jewelry they had to leave behind, when they fled the area subjected to disaster. They could not care less about their family surviving. They are more bothered about their precious material things.

It takes all sorts to make the world, but when disaster strikes, nobody can afford to have whiners and moaners around.

Imagine if the Mayflower was filled up with effete aristocrats fleeing the old world to make a life in the New World. They would embark on Plymouth Rock and asked their valets to dust their coats before they minced out to greet the natives, because they did not want to get their lily white hands dusty and dirty.

One hundred fifty people were aboard the original Mayflower.

The aristocracy of that time was definitely not capable of working with their hands like the indentured hired hands, carpenters, workers, servants, farmers, blacksmiths, dairymaids and other people who landed on Plymouth Rock in order to work and build new lives and better lives for their families in a land of freedom.

I am sometimes taken aback to hear about someone talking about his blue-blooded ancestors coming to America on the Mayflower, instead of being proud of the fact that his pioneering ancestor was possibly an indentured working-class man or a pilgrim possibly fleeing prosecution and the bad social conditions in England. They would rather hide their plebeian and working-class ancestry made up of indentured workers and boast about highborn ancestry.

According to many of these families, their ancestors were European and British gentry. All of them had some highborn relative who belonged to English aristocracy, coming over to the New World in the May Flower.

What they do not want to acknowledge ever is that their ancestors belonged to the lower and working classes, were illiterate, yet were trained and useful enough to work with their hands, and build a secure and flourishing social, traditional and cultural life for them

These brave pioneers definitely did not hanker for the land they had left behind them, where they would slave in sweatshops in order to keep body and soul alive or be prosecuted because of their religion or beliefs.

But their descendants would rather hanker back to genteel delusions of ancestral prosperity and grandeur. And they were proud of the fact that their high-class and noble ancestors came from the Old World. This is the normal human attitude which one takes, when talking about great achievements done by mortals seeking safety and a good life for his family. He would rather play it down and try to hide or forget it.

But human nature being what it is, this exodus can be deemed a traumatic emotional catastrophe, for a person who has to leave a place which is familiar to him. Especially if he has been born in that area and has not traveled away from the land of his roots. This in itself shows courage of a high degree.

But that is a sort of moral and physical courage which is seen very rarely in people of the 21st century. A majority of us are definitely not adventurous, so the mere thought that we have to leave a place, which we consider unfamiliar, is enough to make us break into cold sweat.

That is why people in authority trying to evacuate people living in an area which may be subjected to potential disaster in the coming days, find them adamant. They are going to stay there, come hell and high water. The earthquake or cyclone may pass them by. They are going to take their chances. They are definitely not going to move. If they are evacuated by force, they come back and thus are swept away in the floods, cyclones, or killed in the earthquake.

Why are people so foolish, you may ask? Why do not they try to adapt themselves to changed circumstances? Why do not they try to make a new life of their own, after their previous one has been destroyed irrevocably?

That is because man hates change. Man hates trying something else, especially when he has spent his life building something in one particular area. He would rather take the line of least resistance and die in the place which he considers familiar rather than go to another area where he has to start a new life among people who he thinks may not welcome him and his family.

Now why do I say that? This is natural instinct coming down from time immemorial, and inbuilt in man. Anything not very familiar to him is something of which he has to be cautious. I am putting this down to basic tribal instinct coming down the ages. He knows that if he goes into an unfamiliar area, the people of that tribe living there for centuries are going to wonder whether it is safe having him and his family around. Are they going to contribute to the safety of the community? Are they potential troublemakers? Can they be assimilated in society?

Their natural instinct is – we do not want them here. Your natural instinct is – we do not want to be here. And so the natural instinctive conflict continues.

So this natural prejudice is going to persist even in a supposedly technically advanced world of the 21st century, because our human genes concentrate more on protection of our families as our first priority. And it is going to be, the Neanderthals are moving on to Pithecanthropus land. Do we throw them out? Or do we wait to see what they intend to do?

When people who are been subjected to a natural disaster face this sort of natural prejudice, it is instinctive that they fall back to their own traditional culture, beliefs, and customs as a sort of defense mechanism. Also, they have to learn a completely new way of life. So is it any surprise that they still cling to the dreams of when we go back, we are going to do this and that. They do not want to accept the fact that one way of life has been completely destroyed and they have to start something new.

Training Your Family for Survival

Items in your camping gear can be excellent additions to your survival kit.

When I was a child, my father used to take us hiking into deep jungles and taught us how to navigate by the position of the sun. This not only gave us a taste for adventure, but it also gave us the feeling that even though we were children, we knew how to live off the land, and would survive in cases of disaster. We also grew up to be really tough, self-sufficient and self-confident varmints.

The natives of this area taught us about good fruit, vegetables and herbs to eat. We also tried eating insects like red ants –sour in taste and delicious – and snakes – like chicken and very tasty. If a person makes up his mind to eat something which he knows is nourishing, he is going to enjoy it. If our ancestors lived off the land and ate herbivorous insects, bear, snakes, and monkeys, both in the East and West, why cannot we?

Nyaaa, I want a pizza. At least I know what is in it.

The day of adventuring is gone!

We also learned by sheer luck that if we overturned some rocks in the flowing water in the jungle, we could find caches of wild mangoes, collected by the natives and kept there for cooling.

We fished for crabs and fishes the traditional way, coming down centuries. We learned how to make fire by rubbing a stick in a hole. These natives still have one eternal fire burning in a sacred place, which their ancestors started after lightning struck a tree. According to them, this was the gift of the gods and it had to be kept fed down the ages. This fire must be about 3000 years old or more.

 We learned how to climb trees and fall out of them. We learned how to run and how to stand still when necessary. We learned when to yell – when one is ready to fight or attack – and when not to yell – when one does not want anybody or anything to know about our presence –. [3]

Now this sort of adventurous survival technique is definitely not being taught by parents to their children, because unfortunately they know nothing about it.

And so many of us are going to find ourselves very ill-prepared to face disaster, because we have been so coddled and cushioned that we are going to sulk if we do not have pizza for dinner or access to Facebook, because the lines are down while our world crumbles around us.

During air hostess training of my students, I noticed one who was a cut above the rest. In fact, she went from strength to strength every day, and when I asked her how she had everything streamlined, she said that she went home and practiced until all the moves came instinctive.

She knew exactly what to do when, and once when I put her through some trials with actions to trip her up, she used her own ingenuity, creativity and then continued with what she had learned. She is now working for Lufthansa. So training till your actions are second nature is essential.

Step-by-step training comes in this way –

---

[3] For those who want really in-depth knowledge – get some good survival technique books free at

http://www.thesurvivalistblog.net/top-14-survival-downloads/

I know they are army based, but there are some techniques which you can adapt for yourself and your family.

In case of emergency, who does what and when. Who carries what?

This includes grabbing emergency bags and supplies and exiting the area.

The next step is the place of rendezvous, if the family breaks up.

Get the family to reach the rendezvous place. It may be somewhere outside. It also has to be somewhere in your city, in a place which all of you know, and is easily accessible.

How to get there? Look at all the routes and get there. Make it an adventure. The person reaching that place first needs to have his/her efforts appreciated.

You may want to download a practical PDF for family and disaster planning in the Appendix.

This is definitely going to give you more information on practical things you need to do when faced with disaster.

Also remember that once disaster strikes, you need to be prepared to be evacuated. Do not go running outside to see what happened and to whom. You may find it difficult to get back home and to relative safety.

Practice Building a Shelter Outdoors

Choose dry and well-drained ground, which is free from rocks and reasonably flat. Avoid dead trees and loose rocks near your shelter. They may fall on your Teepee. You need to be near a natural water source, but make sure that your shelter is not built in what could possibly be a riverbed.

You are going to be in danger of being flooded out if you build on a riverbed.

I found this site really amazing. I learned some tricks I did not learn from my father or from my commando relatives.

http://boyslife.org/outdoors/3473/taking-shelter/

Boys are going to enjoy this activity.

Remember to place leaves and pine needles on the ground, because the moment you lie down, you are going to lose body heat.

Food to Survive

Rainwater collected on leaves is going to be the best drink for you, if you find yourself in a tropical forest area.

Living off the land is not something with which people are very comfortable, especially when they are told to eat grasshoppers and grubs. So you may want to make granola energy bars with nuts and oatmeal.

If you like cooking and experimenting a bit, try out this URL for granola recipes with honey and even those no bake recipes

http://allrecipes.com/recipe/granola-energy-bars/morerecipeslikethis.aspx

Pemmican

This food has been used down the ages and it can keep for years without refrigeration.

I cannot improve on these recipes given on this site.

http://www.wildernesscollege.com/pemmican-recipes.html

Also, I learned how to dry meat in the desiccator for eight hours in their first recipe. Also, if you want to make biltong- the URL is in the Appendix.

Biltong makes one of the best survival foods, like dried meat jerky or pemmican. It takes two or three days to make this, but you are going to get a dish which keeps.

Disaster Management Classes – Yes or No?

Should you take disaster management classes? It depends on whether you have $500 to spend with a professional teaching you how to survive in the wilderness. This training and experience cannot be compressed in two days of training.

However, if your city has disaster training classes held by the local Red Cross, by all means do take part in it, and encourage your friends, colleagues and family members to do so too.

Make the Boy Scout motto your own – Be Prepared.

Conclusion

This book begins our disaster management series and gives you an introduction to disasters. You have got tips and techniques which are going to come in useful for disaster management here. Every situation is going to be different so you need to know how to adapt. But the practical tips given in the PDFs and in the URLs can be adapted by anybody with a little bit of enterprise, enthusiasm and intelligence.

Remember, it is better to be safe than to be sorry. Also, an attitude of this cannot happen to me, is definitely not something which you want to cultivate in the 21st century. The struggle for Life and survival are part of the natural instincts inbuilt in man along with other sapient beings. So the struggle for survival between man and man and man and beast is going to continue as long as the earth survives.

So learn about disaster management and start building a survival kit right now.

Appendix

Family disaster plans

www.co.san-diego.ca.us/oes/docs/**Family**DisasterPlan.pdf

Making Biltong the traditional way

https://www.youtube.com/watch?v=wGF0GXhD2Ak

Check out some of the other Prepping and Survival Series books at Amazon.com

Prepping and Survival Series on Amazon

Live Long and Prosper!

Author Bio

Dueep Jyot Singh is a Management and IT Professional who managed to gather Postgraduate qualifications in Management and English and Degrees in Science, French and Education while pursuing different enjoyable career options like being an hospital administrator, IT,SEO and HRD Database Manager/ trainer, movie , radio and TV scriptwriter, theatre artiste and public speaker, lecturer in French, Marketing and Advertising, ex-Editor of Hearts On Fire (now known as Solstice) Books Missouri USA, advice columnist and cartoonist, publisher and Aviation School trainer, ex-moderator on Medico.in, banker, student councilor ,travelogue writer … among other things!

One fine morning, she decided that she had enough of killing herself by Degrees and went back to her first love -- writing. It's more enjoyable! She already has 48 published academic and 14 fiction- in- different- genre books under her belt.

When she is not designing websites or making Graphic design illustrations for clients , she is browsing through old bookshops hunting for treasures, of which she has an enviable collection – including R.L. Stevenson, O.Henry, Dornford Yates, Maurice Walsh, De Maupassant, Victor Hugo, Sapper, C.N. Williamson, "Bartimeus" and the crown of her collection- Dickens "The Old Curiosity Shop," and so on… Just call her "Renaissance Woman" - collecting herbal remedies, acting like Universal Helping Hand/Agony Aunt, or escaping to her dear mountains for a bit of exploring, collecting herbs and plants, and trekking.

Check out some of the other JD-Biz Publishing books

Gardening Series on Amazon

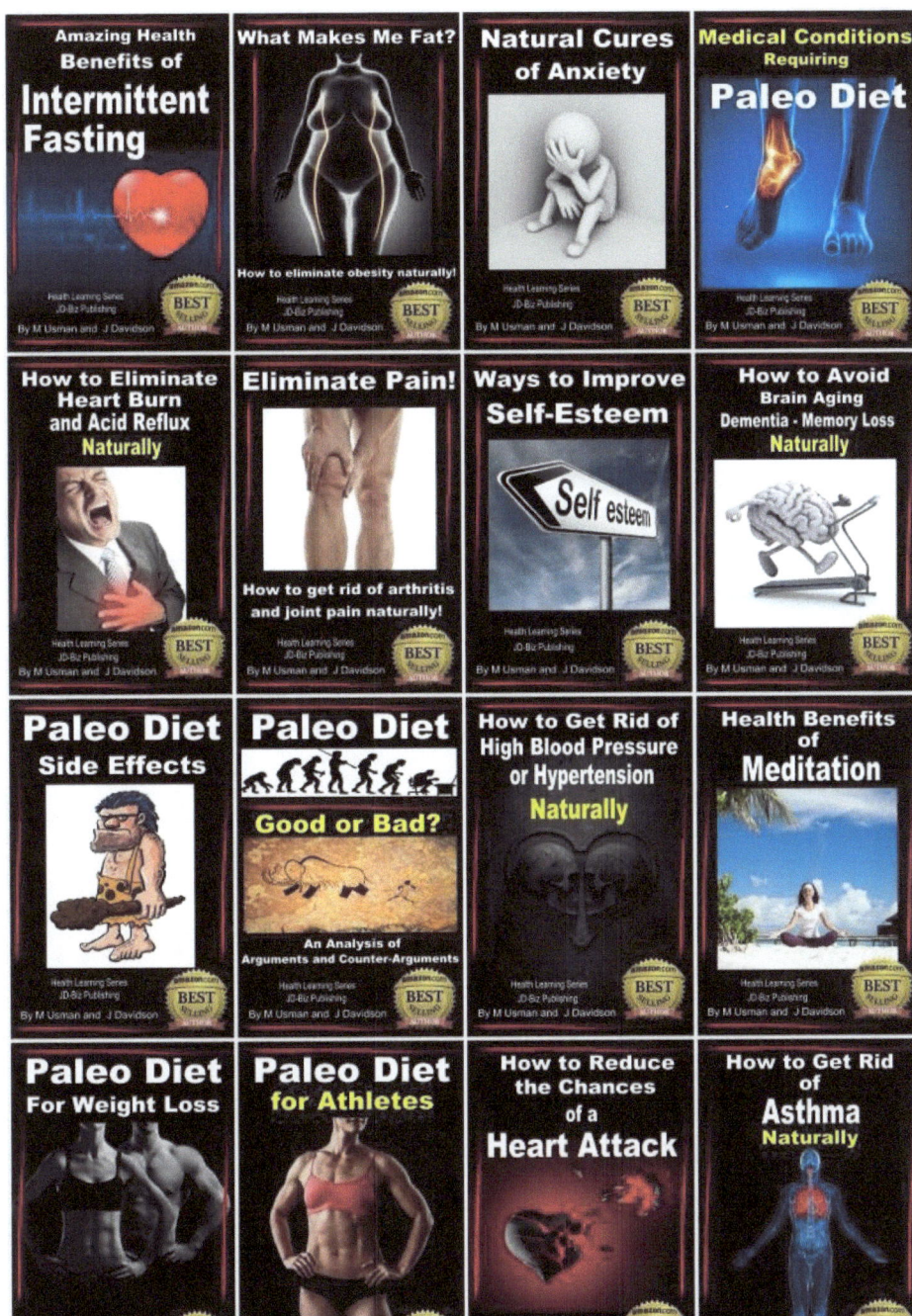

Amazing Animal Book Series

Learn To Draw Series

How to Build and Plan Books

Entrepreneur Book Series

Our books are available at

1. Amazon.com

2. Barnes and Noble

3. Itunes

4. Kobo

5. Smashwords

6. Google Play Books

Download Free Books!

http://MendonCottageBooks.com

Publisher

JD-Biz Corp

P O Box 374

Mendon, Utah 84325

http://www.jd-biz.com/